CONTENTS

A limited number of German Jewish children were allowed to emigrate to Britain, in 1938.

THE GAS CHAMBERS

It is May 1944. A steam engine pulling a line of sealed goods wagons stops alongside a platform. There are German officers in the uniform of the elite SS (Schutzstaffel) standing or strolling about. Some carry whips or have snarling dogs on leads. Jewish prisoners are also present, ashen-faced, in blue-striped prison garb. They step forward to open the doors of the wagons. Inside are over two thousand Hungarian Jews.

Jews being transported eastwards were told that they were going to forced labour or resettlement camps. In fact, their fate on arrival was most likely to be instant death.

These people have travelled for days without food or water. They are half starved and delirious. They do not know where they have arrived. The name of the place is, in Polish, Oswiecim – in German, Auschwitz. Ordered out of the wagons, they tumble down on to the platform, clutching their belongings. They are instructed to put their belongings down, and the Jewish prisoners begin to collect the suitcases and bags. SS officers walk among the new arrivals, selecting a few of the able-bodied with a gesture of the thumb.

Most of the Jews are herded to the left, including all the older men, most of the women and all of the children. The few people picked out by the SS are driven to the right. It is not explained to them, but they have been selected for work, and will have a small chance of survival. Sometimes a man is chosen but his wife and child are not. There is panic as they try to say hurried farewells.

NEW PERSPECTIVES

The Holocaust

R. G. GRANT

HODDER
Wayland

an imprint of Hodder Children's Books

First published in Great Britain in 1997
by Wayland Publishers Ltd
Reprinted in 2000 by Hodder Wayland,
an imprint of Hodder Children's Books
© Hodder Wayland 1997

Hodder Children's Books, a division of Hodder Headline Ltd,
338 Euston Road, London NW1 3BH

This book was prepared for Wayland Publishers Ltd
by Ruth Nason.

R.G. Grant asserts his right to be identified as author of this
work, in accordance with the Copyright, Designs and Patents
Act 1988.

Series editor: Alex Woolf
Series design: Stonecastle Graphics
Book design: LNbooks, Houghton Regis, Bedfordshire

British Library Cataloguing in Publication Data
Grant, R.G.
    The Holocaust. – (New perspectives)
    1. Holocaust, Jewish (1939-1945) – Juvenile literature
    I. Title
    940.5'318

ISBN 0 7502 2601 3

Printed and bound in Italy by G. Canale & C.S.p.A., Turin

Cover photos: Survivors of
Auschwitz during the first
hours of the camp's
liberation by the Soviet
army, January 1945; part of
the Holocaust memorial in
Miami, Florida.

Page 1: A bench 'for
Aryans only'; an early sign
of the Nazi regime's
persecution of Jewish
people.

Acknowledgements

The Author and Publishers thank the following for their permission
to reproduce photographs: Angela Wood: page 35; Camera Press:
pages 4, 6, 30, 31, 37, 39, 42, 43, 51, 52, 56 (bottom); Hulton-Getty
Picture Collection: pages 1, 3, 8, 12, 13, 18, 19, 22, 25, 26, 28, 32, 46,
54 (top), 55; Museum of Danish Resistance 1940-45: page 48;
Popperfoto: cover (left) and pages 20, 23, 24, 33, 36, 40, 41 (top), 53;
Robert Harding Picture Library: cover (right) and pages 5 (top), 59;
Topham Picturepoint: 5 (bottom), 7, 10, 14, 16, 17, 21, 34, 41 (bottom),
45, 47, 54 (bottom), 56 (top). The maps on pages 9, 11 and 15 are
adapted from maps in Martin Gilbert, *The Dent Atlas of Jewish
History* (copyright Martin Gilbert).

66 Journey to Auschwitz

In February 1944, 650 Jews from northern Italy were packed into sealed freight wagons for transportation to Auschwitz. The journey lasted four days and nights, in unheated wagons with temperatures below freezing. The Jews were given no food or drink. A chemist, Primo Levi, was one of those on the train. He later described the journey:

'We suffered from thirst and cold; at every stop we clamoured for water, or even a handful of snow, but we were rarely heard; the soldiers of the escort drove off anybody who tried to approach the convoy. Two young mothers, nursing their children, groaned night and day, begging for water ... The hours of darkness were nightmares without end.' (From *If This Is A Man*) 99

An Auschwitz wagon at Yad V'Shem, a museum of the Holocaust in Israel.

New arrivals at Auschwitz station.

Tragic separation

When they got out of the train, people selected for work were separated from others of their family. Of course, they had no idea that these others were to be taken straight to the gas chambers. Sometimes hasty farewells were possible. Richard Glazar, a prisoner at Treblinka, recalled how a fellow prisoner, Hans, spoke of his pain on being separated from his wife and son:

"'I can only think of my wife and boy," said Hans ... "My little boy had curly hair and soft skin – soft on his cheeks like on his bottom – that same smooth soft skin. When we got off the train he said he was cold, and I said to his mother, 'I hope he won't catch a cold.' A cold. When they separated us he waved to me ...'" (Quoted in G. Sereny, *Into That Darkness*)

An incinerator for burning bodies, at Belsen concentration camp.

The crowd of people on the left are moved along a path between neat grass borders. They can see flames from tall chimneys nearby and an awful smell fills the air – it is the stench of burning bodies, but they do not know it. They are forced down some steps into a large bare room. Signs in various languages say: Baths and Disinfection Room. The Jews are told to undress and leave their clothes on numbered hooks. They are advised to remember the number, so they can reclaim their clothes after the shower, and they are assured that they will have a cup of coffee when the disinfection is over.

Naked, they are directed into another brightly lit room. Most behave calmly until the door is sealed shut behind them and the lights are switched off.

Undressing for death

The commandant of Auschwitz camp, Rudolf Hoess, wrote his memoirs in prison after the war. He described the process of tricking the Jews into entering the gas chambers. The victims were told that they had to undress to be washed and disinfected:

'It was most important that the whole process of arriving and undressing should take place in an atmosphere of the greatest possible calm. People reluctant to take off their clothes had to be helped by those of their companions who had already undressed, or by men of the Special Detachment [Jewish prisoners] ... The smaller children usually cried because of the strangeness of being undressed in this fashion, but when their mothers or members of the Special Detachment comforted them, they became calm and entered the gas chambers, playing or joking with one another and carrying their toys.' (From *Commandant of Auschwitz*)

Rudolf Hoess, commandant of Auschwitz, on trial before Poland's Supreme National Tribunal, March 1947.

A member of the SS drops some powder through a vent into the crowded chamber. It turns to poison gas, which begins to fill the chamber. Another SS officer watches impassively through a spy hole in the sealed door. He sees screaming, twisted faces as the victims clamber over one another in a desperate fight for air.

A few minutes later, everything is silent. The doors of the gas chamber are opened and Jewish prisoners in their striped uniforms move in. Their dreadful task is to wash down the bodies with hosepipes and then pull them one by one to an elevator. This carries the bodies to a crematorium on the level above.

Last struggle for life

Dr Miklos Nyiszli, a Hungarian prisoner who survived Auschwitz, described the scene inside a gas chamber when the doors were opened after a mass killing:

'The bodies were not lying here and there throughout the room but piled in a mass to the ceiling. The reason for this was that the gas first inundated the lower layers of air and rose but slowly toward the ceiling. This forced the victims to trample one another in a frantic effort to escape the gas ... I noticed that the bodies of the women, the children and the aged were at the bottom of the pile; at the top, the strongest.' (Quoted in O. Friedrich, *The Kingdom of Auschwitz*)

Before the bodies are burned, other Jewish prisoners have to cut the hair off the corpses' heads and yank out gold teeth from their mouths with pliers. Then the bodies are loaded into the furnace. Within a few hours of arrival, all that is left of most of the people on the train is ashes.

Allied troops liberating the concentration camps in 1945 found piles of clothes of murdered prisoners and forced labourers.

Plan for genocide

Massacres like the one just described occurred thousands of times in 1941-4, during the Second World War. Under the rule of the Nazi dictator Adolf Hitler, Germany set up six extermination camps: Auschwitz-Birkenau, Chelmno, Belzec, Sobibor, Treblinka and Majdanek. Between them, these camps gassed over three million Jews.

The concentration camps and extermination camps set up by the Nazis.

Further east, in German-occupied parts of the Soviet Union, the Germans killed more than two million Jews, most of them shot and buried in pits. In addition, hundreds of thousands of Jews were worked to death or died of mistreatment, starvation and disease in concentration camps and ghettos.

The Jews were not the only people to suffer at the hands of the Nazis. Millions of Poles and Russians were their victims. As well as Jews, gypsies, homosexuals and the mentally ill were all marked down for extermination. Many thousands of forced labourers from all over Europe and political opponents of the Nazis – liberals, socialists and communists – died in the camps.

But the Jewish Holocaust is the most shocking and unprecedented expression of the evil of the German state under the Nazis. The Nazis planned to seek out and kill every Jewish man, woman and child living in Europe. They made this plan because of an absurd belief that Jews were a deadly threat to the German people. Jewish people had done nothing to provoke their bitter fate. They were the innocent victims of a paranoid delusion.

It was only because Europe was liberated from Nazi rule by the Allied armies of Britain, the USA and the Soviet Union that the Nazis did not succeed in completing the act of genocide. This book is the story of the Nazis' attempt to destroy the European Jews.

Heinrich Himmler, head of the SS.

66 'A page of glory'

Hitler gave the task of exterminating the Jews to the SS, led by Heinrich Himmler. In October 1943, in a speech to senior SS officers, Himmler described the Holocaust as 'a page of glory in our history which is never to be written'. He went on:

'We had the moral right, we had the duty ... to destroy this people [the Jews] which wanted to destroy us ... we can say we have fulfilled this most difficult duty for the love of our people. And our spirit, our soul, our character has not suffered injury from it.' (Quoted in M. Gilbert, *The Holocaust*) 99

THE PERSECUTION OF JEWS

Jews in Europe had long been a target for hatred and persecution. In the Middle Ages, when nearly all other Europeans were Christian, Jews stood out as an alien people with a different religion and different customs. In many medieval European cities, Jewish people were forced to live in their own areas, known as ghettos. They were banned from many kinds of work, and so some Jews became moneylenders. People who owed them money hated them even more.

Jewish ghettos, 1215-1870.

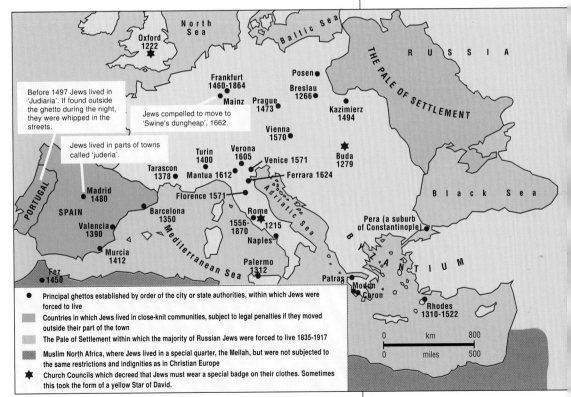

Before 1497 Jews lived in 'Judiaria'. If found outside the ghetto during the night, they were whipped in the streets.

Jews compelled to move to 'Swine's dungheap', 1662.

Jews lived in parts of towns called 'juderia'.

- Principal ghettos established by order of the city or state authorities, within which Jews were forced to live
- Countries in which Jews lived in close-knit communities, subject to legal penalties if they moved outside their part of the town
- The Pale of Settlement within which the majority of Russian Jews were forced to live 1835-1917
- Muslim North Africa, where Jews lived in a special quarter, the Mellah, but were not subjected to the same restrictions and indignities as in Christian Europe
- ★ Church Councils which decreed that Jews must wear a special badge on their clothes. Sometimes this took the form of a yellow Star of David.

Often, Christians in the Middle Ages made wild accusations against Jews. They blamed them for the crucifixion of Jesus and accused them of murdering Christian children in secret ceremonies. Jews were

This illustration of the Jews of Cologne being burned alive appeared in a book printed in Nuremberg in 1493.

blamed for infecting the Christian population with diseases such as the plague. Occasionally, Christians savagely attacked Jews and massacred whole communities. Some Christian rulers drove all Jews out of their lands.

'Bitter worms'

Hatred of Jews had deep roots in German culture. The religious reformer Martin Luther (1483-1546) was the founder of German Protestantism. He is a heroic figure in German history, but he was intensely anti-Semitic. Writing in 1543, he described the Jews as 'poisonous bitter worms':

'... they hold us Christians captive in our country ... mock us and spit on us, because we work and permit them to be lazy squires who own us and our realm; they are therefore our lords, we their servants ...' (Quoted in M. Gilbert, *The Holocaust*)

Luther wrote that Jews' houses and synagogues should be destroyed, and that they should be driven out of Germany 'for all time'.

Tolerance and assimilation

From the seventeenth century, the position of Jews in Western Europe began to improve. By the late nineteenth century, the medieval massacres were a half-forgotten nightmare. Jews had been given equal legal and political rights, and were increasingly integrated into the rest of society. There were some marriages between Jews and Christians. Old prejudice still lurked beneath the surface but, on the whole, Jews mixed on equal terms with non-Jews.

In Germany, united as a powerful nation state in 1871, more and more Jews became educated and successful. They were still banned from a few areas of society – it was almost impossible for a Jew to become an officer in the army, for example. But Jews flourished as doctors, lawyers, businessmen, scientists, journalists, artists and musicians. Some adopted the Christian faith.

When the First World War broke out in 1914, Jews showed that they were as patriotic as anyone else in the countries where they lived. German Jews fought for Germany, Austrian Jews for Austria, French Jews for France, British Jews for Britain. About 100,000 Jews served in the German army during the war, and many won medals for their bravery.

Whitechapel Road, London, 26 June 1919: a demonstration against the pogroms in Poland.

Hatred survives

But anti-Semitism – hatred of Jews – had never died out. In the Russian Empire, including parts of Poland and the Ukraine, the mass of Jews still lived in traditional communities, surrounded by hostile Christians. Their freedom was limited and they were terrorized by pogroms – organized attacks allowed by the authorities. In 1919, about 60,000 Jews were massacred by Ukrainian nationalists and others.

The back cover of a racist magazine from 1922 asked: 'Germans. Who should lead? Who should be duke?'

Thousands of Eastern European Jews fled to Western Europe and the USA both before and after the First World War.

Even in Western Europe, hatred of Jews was still rife. During the nineteenth century, right-wing nationalists developed a supposedly 'scientific' anti-Semitism, based on race rather than on religion. Such views were especially popular in Germany and Austria. German nationalists claimed that the German people were superior because they belonged to the 'Aryan' race of blond, blue-eyed warriors. Jews were portrayed as an inferior, evil race who plotted to corrupt the pure Aryan blood of the Germans and the pure German spirit.

Even before the First World War, extreme nationalists called for Germany to be cleared of Jews. Such views were expressed by important German cultural figures including the composer Richard Wagner and his friends. Anti-Semitism appealed to ordinary Germans who envied the successful careers of integrated Jews, or resented the arrival of thousands of poverty-stricken Jews fleeing from Eastern Europe.

'Crush the vermin'

Scholar and philosopher Paul de Lagarde expressed ideas that were typical of German anti-Semitism in the late nineteenth century. He saw Jews as a hidden enemy in the body of Germany, like a malignant disease. In 1887, de Lagarde described how he hated both the Jews and

'those who – for humanitarian reasons! – defend the Jews, or are too cowardly to crush the vermin ... Where such a concentration of decay has accumulated as in Europe's Jewry, medicine can succeed only where a surgical incision has first removed the source of infection.' (Quoted in H. Graml, *Anti-Semitism in the Third Reich*)

Germany defeated

After the First World War, anti-Semitism received a huge boost in Germany. The war ended in November 1918 with the defeat of Germany by the Allies. This defeat came as a profound shock to many Germans. They could not believe that the German army had lost the war. Instead, they accepted the idea that was put around that the army had been 'stabbed in the back' – betrayed by people on the home front, especially socialist politicians and revolutionaries, who had agreed to surrender when the army could have fought on. Some of these people they blamed were Jews.

Life was hard in Germany in the years after the defeat. The country was humiliated by the peace terms imposed by the Allies in the Treaty of Versailles. In 1923, inflation raged unchecked. Money became worthless and people's life savings were wiped out. At the end of the 1920s, when it seemed as if things might be returning to normal, the country was plunged into an economic depression. By 1932, two out of every five German workers were unemployed.

Anti-Semitism in Europe, 1917-33.

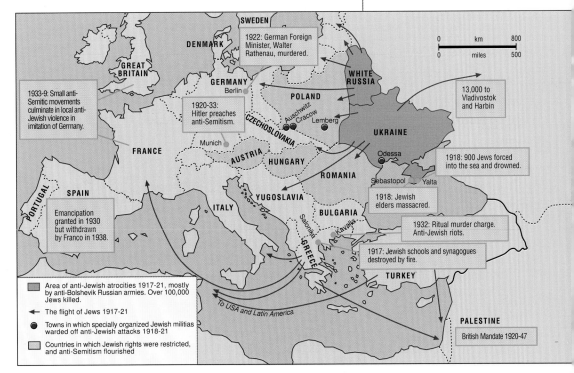

Adolf Hitler, 1889-1945.
He told the German people
that all their misfortunes
were the Jews' fault.

The rise of Hitler

Adolf Hitler, the leader of the National Socialist (Nazi) Party, told the Germans that there was one hidden enemy responsible for all their misfortunes: the Jews. Like most German soldiers who fought in the First World War, Hitler had been shattered by Germany's defeat. He adapted traditional anti-Semitic ideas to explain why the defeat had happened. According to Hitler, Germany had been the victim of a Jewish conspiracy. Jewish capitalists in the Allied countries had financed the war, and Jewish socialists and communists inside Germany had been responsible for the 'stab in the back' against the army.

Hitler claimed that Germany's main enemies in the post-war world were American capitalists and the Bolshevik (communist) government of the Soviet Union. According to him, both of these were Jewish. If the Germans were to be strong again, Hitler said, the Jews must be defeated both inside and outside Germany.

Keeping pure

Adolf Hitler believed that German Aryans were engaged in a struggle for survival against the subhuman, but cunning, Jewish race. He portrayed the Jews as 'bacilli', or germs, threatening to poison German blood. In his book *Mein Kampf*, Hitler described the sexuality of Jews as a threat to the racial purity of German women:

'The black-haired Jewish youth lies in wait for hours on end, satanically glaring at and spying on the unsuspicious girl whom he plans to seduce, adulterating her blood and removing her from the bosom of her own people. The Jew uses every possible means to undermine the racial foundations of a subjugated people ... For as long as a people remain racially pure ... they can never be overcome by the Jew.'

Jews for Germany

Many Jews were German patriots and deeply resented the Nazis' claim that they were disloyal to Germany. A Jewish newspaper wrote in 1933:

'The Nazis ... designate the Jews as "enemies of the state". That designation is incorrect. The Jews are not enemies of the state. The German Jews desire and wish for the rise of Germany, for which they have always invested, to the best of their knowledge, all their resources, and that is what they wish to continue to do.' (Quoted in R. Hilberg, *The Destruction of the European Jews*)

Jews were not the only people that Hitler despised. He regarded all Slavs – the majority of the inhabitants of the Soviet Union, Poland, Czechoslovakia, Bulgaria and Yugoslavia – as an inferior race destined to be used as slaves by the German Aryans. He also believed in eugenics, the theory that a nation could be improved by selective breeding. He thought that people with undesirable genetic material should be stopped from having children, or simply killed. In this group he included people with mental illnesses, homosexuals, and anyone who was unwilling to work. But no other people were regarded by Hitler and his followers as quite as evil or as dangerous as the Jews.

Hitler had a genius for propaganda and political organization. He built the Nazi Party into the single biggest political party in Germany. He promised strong government to restore order and make the country powerful again. In January 1933 he was appointed chancellor of Germany and, after elections in March, the Nazis took control of parliament. For the first time in the modern era, a West European country had a government openly dedicated to the persecution of Jews.

After the Nazis came to power in the 1930s, they used the cinema to spread anti-Semitic ideas. This is a poster for a 1937 film, *The Eternal Jew*.

THE NAZIS IN POWER

When the Nazis came to power in 1933, there were about 500,000 Jews in Germany – less than one per cent of the population. The Nazi stormtroopers, the SA (Sturmabteilung), Hitler's brown-shirted private army, immediately set about intimidating this vulnerable minority. Jews were beaten up at random and Jewish property was attacked. Jews were among those arrested to be sent to the first concentration camps. In April 1933, the Nazi government ordered a one-day boycott of Jewish shops. The stormtroopers harassed people who broke the boycott.

April 1933.
The large notice says: 'Germans! Defend yourselves! Don't buy from Jews!' Stormtroopers are fixing labels to the window saying that entry to the shop is forbidden.

But Hitler and the other Nazi leaders knew they had to proceed with caution. German public opinion was not ready in 1933 for extreme measures against Jews. Many respectable Germans disapproved of the storm-troopers' strongarm tactics. The Nazis were also concerned about international opinion, which they were not yet strong enough to ignore. So the stormtroopers were reined in, and persecution of the Jews developed only gradually, as the Nazis' confidence grew and their hold over Germany strengthened.

The first five years of Nazi rule

First Jews were banned from the civil service and from journalism. Then they were progressively excluded from higher education and from the armed forces. Jewish scientists such as Albert Einstein were

driven into exile. So were prominent architects, authors and composers. German schools, newspapers and cinemas became vehicles for outrageous anti-Semitic propaganda. In 1935 the notorious Nuremberg Laws deprived Jews of German citizenship. Jews who had thought of themselves throughout their lives as Germans were now aliens in their own country. New marriages between Jews and 'Aryans' were banned.

1935: two people paraded through the streets as discouraging examples. The woman's placard says: 'I am the greatest swine and only get mixed up with Jews.' The man's says: 'As a Jew, I take only German girls up to my room.'

Jewish pride

Many Jews in Germany no longer practised the Jewish religion or kept Jewish traditions. They thought of themselves as Germans. After the Nazi-imposed boycott of Jewish businesses in April 1933, a Jewish journalist, Robert Weltsch, called on Jews to take pride in their identity. Jews had been forced to admit their Jewishness by stormtroopers painting a yellow Star of David on their windows. But they should not be depressed by this, Weltsch wrote:

'They meant to dishonour us ... Jews, take it upon yourselves, that Star of David, and honour it anew.' (Quoted in M. Gilbert, *The Holocaust*)

March 1938: Austrian Nazis cheered German troops.

In the first five years of Nazi rule, over 100,000 German Jews emigrated, driven out by Nazi pressure.

Ritual murder

The Nazi newspaper *Der Sturmer* specialized in extreme anti-Semitic propaganda. It revived medieval images of Jews. For example, in 1937, it described how Jews stole Christian children for ritual murder:

'The blood of the victims is to be tapped by force. On Passover it is to be used in wine and matzohs ... the head of the family then says "Thus we ask God to send the ten plagues to all enemies of the Jewish faith." Then they eat, and at the end the head of the family exclaims, "May all Gentiles perish, as the child whose blood is contained in the bread and wine."'

Many Germans believed such false accusations against the Jews.

Who is a Jew?

Jews were so fully integrated into German society that the Nazis met problems in defining who was and was not Jewish. In November 1935 a decree stated that:

'A Jew is anyone who is descended from at least three grandparents who are racially full Jews.'

The decree also defined complex categories of Jewish half-caste – those who had fewer than three Jewish grandparents, but some Jewish blood. These might count as full Jews if, for example, they married a Jew or professed the Jewish religion.

Jews married to 'Aryan' Germans, especially those who had children, were often exempted from the worst anti-Jewish laws. Also, Jews who had served in the German army in the First World War were often slightly better treated.

Anti-Jewish measures toughen

In 1938, Nazi policy towards the Jews toughened. In March, the German army moved into Austria, joining it to the German Reich in the 'Anschluss' (union). Cheering crowds greeted Hitler in the Austrian capital, Vienna. The Anschluss was followed immediately by an onslaught on Austria's 180,000 Jews. They were beaten up and subjected to public humiliation. Passers-by watched passively as stormtroopers forced elderly Jews to scrub streets on their hands and knees.

Jews were now driven out of almost all employment. Throughout the Nazi-ruled Reich, Jewish doctors were no longer allowed to treat 'Aryan' patients, or Jewish lawyers to have 'Aryan' clients. Jewish businesses had to be sold to 'Aryan' competitors for next to nothing.

For Austrian Jews, the arrival of the German troops was nothing to cheer about.

Night of broken glass

A rabbi in Düsseldorf, Dr Max Eschenbacher, described how he was terrorized by the SA on Krystallnacht, the night of 9-10 November 1938.

'The street in front of the building was full of SA people. In a moment they were upstairs and had forced the hall door ... They forced their way into our apartment with a chorus of "Revenge for Paris!" and "Down with the Jews!" They pulled sledgehammers out of sacks, and in a moment breaking furniture cracked, and panes of glass in sideboards and windows smashed. Then the fellows threatened me with their clenched fists. One of them grabbed me and screamed at me to get downstairs. I was convinced I was about to be beaten to death ... I saw that the street was covered with books, papers, documents and letters which had been thrown out of my windows. My typewriter lay smashed to pieces on the street.' (Quoted in M. Burleigh and W. Wipperman, *The Racial State*)

In November 1938, persecution reached a new pitch. On 7 November an official at the German embassy in Paris was shot. The assassin was Hirschel Grynszpan, the son of a Polish Jew who had recently been expelled from Germany under brutal circumstances. Two days later Hitler's propaganda chief, Joseph Goebbels, called for nationwide revenge against the Jews. The pogrom that followed was called Krystallnacht, the 'night of broken glass'. Stormtroopers set fire to almost 200 synagogues. Jews were beaten in the street, and their homes and shops were broken into and looted. About 90 Jews were killed. Over 20,000 were arrested and carried off to

Damage caused on Krystallnacht, to a shop in Berlin selling bedding.

concentration camps, where many more died over the following months. To add to the humiliation of the Jews, they were then forced to pay a heavy fine as 'compensation' for the embassy killing.

The Krystallnacht attacks provoked a storm of international protest. Some Germans also objected to such disorder and thuggish behaviour. But the German and Austrian Jews were now totally isolated and helpless. They had no jobs or businesses. They were excluded from cinemas, bathing areas and sports facilities. Their children could no longer attend schools or universities. Their only hope was emigration.

Leaving Germany

The Nazis were not opposed to the Jews emigrating, as long as they left their property behind. A Central Office for Jewish Emigration was set up in Vienna, under an SS officer, Adolf Eichmann. But the countries the Jews wanted to emigrate to were less than keen to receive them.

A synagogue in Berlin, set on fire by stormtroopers on Krystallnacht.

An increasing number of Jews were entering Palestine, which was controlled by the British. The British wanted to stop the Jews from going there because the arrival of so many was stirring the local Arab population to revolt. The USA was operating strict quota systems under which only a certain number of immigrants were allowed to enter the country each year.

In April 1939, the Germans took over Czechoslovakia, which had a large Jewish population. Britain and the USA were then even more worried at the number of Jews who might want to emigrate.

Fleeing from Germany

Emigrating from Nazi Germany was often heartbreaking because people were separated from members of their families who could not obtain the visas they needed. Eric Lucas left Germany for Britain in 1939. He later described the agony of leaving his parents behind:

'Standing at the window of the train, I was suddenly overcome with a maiming certainty that I would never see my father and mother again. There they stood, lonely, and with the sadness of death ... Now and then my mother would stretch her hand out, as if to grasp mine – but the hand fell back, knowing it could never reach ... As the train pulled out of the station to wheel me to safety, I leant my face against the cold glass of the window, and wept bitterly.' (Quoted in M. Gilbert, *The Holocaust*)

Britain did make one generous gesture, admitting 10,000 German Jewish children in 1938-9. But thousands who could have been saved were left in Nazi hands because of a lack of visas or immigration permits.

By September 1939, about half the Jews under Nazi rule had managed to emigrate. Those left behind knew they faced a bleak future – but could not have imagined how bleak.

One of 500 children from Vienna who arrived at Harwich, England, in December 1938 and were taken to live at a holiday camp in Lowestoft. The youngest child among them was only two years old.

THE FINAL SOLUTION

In September 1939, Germany invaded Poland and this led to the Second World War, as Britain and France declared war on Germany. Under cover of war, the Nazis dared to carry out acts they could never have attempted in peacetime. On the day the war started, Hitler gave an order for the systematic extermination of the German mentally disabled. Many of the people who took part in this 'euthanasia' programme for the gassing of the mentally ill would later transfer to the programme to exterminate the Jews.

In the Warsaw ghetto, men and women were made to stand for long periods with their hands in the air, while they were searched.

The conquest of Poland brought more than three million Polish Jews under Nazi rule. The Polish city of Warsaw alone had a larger Jewish population than the whole German Reich. The conquerors terrorized the Polish Jews with public humiliations, beatings and random killings. They began driving them into crowded ghettos in an area of Poland known as the General Government. German Jews were also deported to these ghettos. To mark them out, Jews were made to wear a yellow Star of David.

Measures were taken to keep the Jews in Warsaw entirely separate. Special bridges were constructed by which Jews had to cross 'Aryan' streets. The bridges were strictly guarded.

By mid-1940, after a series of swift military victories, the Nazis dominated most of Europe. Since they believed that the Jews were a disease and a permanent threat to the German people, they were in no doubt that the areas under their control should be made 'Jew-free'. But how was it to be done? The Nazis considered the possibility of forcing all Jews to emigrate. One plan was to create a 'Jewish homeland' somewhere in Eastern Europe. Another was to send all the Jews to Madagascar, a French island off the coast of southern Africa. But in 1941 both these options were overtaken by a simpler, more direct plan for ending the 'Jewish problem'.

Dying of cold

Conditions were appalling in the overcrowded ghettos set up by the Nazis in Polish cities. In the Warsaw ghetto during the winter of 1941-2, there were severe shortages of food and fuel. Thousands died of cold or starvation. A Jewish writer inside the ghetto, Emanuel Ringelblum, noted one night:

'The most fearful sight is that of freezing children. Little children with bare feet, bare knees and torn clothing stand dumbly in the street weeping. Tonight ... I heard a tot of three or four yammering [crying]. The child will probably be found frozen to death tomorrow morning, a few hours off.'
(Quoted in M. Gilbert, *The Holocaust*)

Was the Holocaust planned in advance?

In a speech on 30 January 1939, Hitler issued a dire warning of what would happen if war broke out:

'If the international Jewish financiers in and outside Europe should succeed in plunging the nations once more into a world war, then the result will not be the Bolshevising of the earth, and thus a victory of Jewry, but the annihilation of the Jewish race in Europe.' (Quoted in M. Burleigh and W. Wipperman, *The Racial State*)

This seems a clear statement that Hitler intended to massacre the Jews if war broke out. But many historians do not believe that Hitler or other Nazi leaders had such a clear-cut long-term plan to kill all European Jews. They think that the Nazis seriously considered forcing all Jews to emigrate, or to resettle in a 'Jewish homeland', and that the idea of physically exterminating the Jews only gradually took over as the war went on. At a certain point, it came to seem the most practical solution to the 'Jewish problem'.

War of extermination

In June 1941, the Germans and their allies invaded the Soviet Union. In the path of the invasion lay about five million Jews in the Baltic States, the Ukraine and Byelorussia. Before the invasion, Hitler told his generals that this was a racial conflict in which the normal rules of war would not apply. They were to be merciless towards the Slavs, and doubly merciless towards Slav communists. Hitler said that special SS units, known as Einsatzgruppen, would travel behind the army, and that their task, in every area the army had conquered, would be to shoot all communist officials, or commissars. But the real order given to the special units was to exterminate all Soviet Jews.

As soon as the invasion got under way, the mass murder of Jews began. The SS played the prime role in these atrocities, but ordinary German army and police units also took part. So did the local population. Lithuanians, Latvians and Ukrainians sometimes took the lead in massacring their local Jewish population.

Thousands of them became tools of the SS, providing militia, police and prison camp guards to aid in the Holocaust.

Many Soviet Jews became partisans, resistance fighters against the Germans in occupied areas of the Soviet Union.

The killing was on a massive scale. At Babi Yar outside Kiev in September 1941, over 33,000 Jews were massacred in two days. They were mown down by machine gun fire and fell into a large ravine, which was then covered with earth to hide the bodies. Killing on this scale occurred in hundreds of towns across the area of German occupation. In place after place, out of Jewish populations of thousands, only a few individuals survived. Some of these fled to join partisan (resistance) groups. Others proved useful as skilled workers for the Germans. A few were hidden by local people.

Feeling no pity

An SS man, Felix Landau, kept a diary while he was serving with a killing squad in the Ukraine. He described his complete lack of feeling at shooting a group of Jews:

'The condemned were given shovels in order to dig their own grave. Two of them were crying ... Curiously, absolutely nothing disturbed me. No pity, nothing ... The women were seized and taken to the edge of the trench, where they turned around. Six of us had to shoot them, divided so three of us aimed at the heart and three at the head. I took the heart ... The last two had to sit on the far edge of the grave so that they would fall in exactly. Then a few corpses were rearranged with a pickaxe, and we began the burial work.' (Quoted in M. Burleigh and W. Wipperman, *The Racial State*)

Shootings in the Ukraine

A German civilian, Hermann Graebe, witnessed the mass murder of Jews in the Ukraine by the SS and Ukrainian militia. He saw Jews taken in trucks from the town of Dubno to a killing ground:

'The people who had got off the trucks – men, women and children of all ages – had to undress under the orders of an SS man, who carried a riding or dog whip. They had to put down their clothes in fixed places, sorted according to shoes, top clothing and underclothing. Without screaming or weeping these people undressed, stood around in family groups, kissed each other, said farewells ... '
(Quoted in J. Carey, *The Faber Book of Reportage*)

Graebe then watched as the Jews were made to climb down into a large pit that was already half full of bodies. Standing or lying on the corpses, they were shot by an SS man with a machine gun.

Although there were some mild protests from army officers, these massacres went on in daylight and to the general knowledge of all. The dead were never counted, but they may have numbered two and a half million. The special unit firing squads probably killed almost as many Jews as died in the gas chambers.

The German army in Russia

Officers and ordinary soldiers in the German army fighting in the Soviet Union knew about the massacres being carried out by the SS firing squads. In an official report on attitudes in the German Sixth Army in December 1941, an officer wrote:

'I had the impression that the shooting of Jews, prisoners of war and even commissars was disapproved of in the officer corps ... It should be noted that the facts of the matter are fully known and that they are much more widely discussed among the officers at the front than was expected.'
(Quoted in H. Graml, *Anti-Semitism in the Third Reich*)

SS second-in-command
Reinhard Heydrich,
photographed in
September 1941.

Although they occasionally complained about what was happening, German officers and soldiers did not take any action to stop the killings. Indeed, many army units themselves carried out massacres of Jews, either under SS orders or on their own initiative.

The Final Solution

For the Nazis, the killings in the Soviet Union were the start of the extermination of the Jews of Europe – which they called the 'Final Solution' (Endlösung) of the Jewish problem. No Jewish man, woman or child was to be allowed to survive. Hitler never issued a written order for the Holocaust to take place. But every leading Nazi was certain that the extermination of the Jews was 'the Führer's wish'.

In July 1941, Hitler's associate Hermann Goering sent an order to Reinhard Heydrich, second-in-command to Heinrich Himmler in the SS. The order told Heydrich 'to make all the necessary organizational and material preparations for a comprehensive solution to the Jewish question in the German sphere of influence in Europe'. In October, Jewish emigration was banned. Europe was now a closed trap for the Jews.

The SS decided on gas as the method of extermination, partly because they felt that shooting was too emotionally distressing for those who had to do the killing. People who had been working on the programme to eradicate the mentally disabled were drafted in to the Final Solution programme because of their knowledge of the use of gas.

Polish Jews were targeted first. In the winter of 1941, thousands were sent to an extermination centre at Chelmno, where gas vans were used to kill them. The exhaust was turned back into the van so that they died of carbon monoxide poisoning while being driven to

The Wannsee Conference

On 20 January 1942, SS leader Reinhard Heydrich chaired a conference in the Wannsee suburb of Berlin. He told leading civil servants from the Ministry of Justice, the Foreign Office and other government departments about the 'Final Solution' to the Jewish problem:

'In pursuance of the final solution, the Jews will be conscripted for labour service in the east under appropriate supervision. Large labour gangs will be formed from those fit for work ... undoubtedly a large number of them will drop out through natural wastage. The remainder who survive – and they will certainly be those who have the greatest powers of endurance – will have to be dealt with accordingly. For if released, they would, as a natural selection of the fittest, form a germ-cell from which the Jewish race could regenerate itself.' (Quoted in M. Burleigh and W. Wipperman, *The Racial State*)

All present understood that Heydrich meant that the Jews were to be annihilated. No one made any protest. All the German civil servants promised their full cooperation in carrying out the Final Solution.

mass graves. Carbon monoxide was also used in gas chambers constructed between autumn 1941 and spring 1942 at Belzec, Majdanek, Sobibor and Treblinka. At Auschwitz, where an extermination centre was added to an existing concentration camp, an insecticide called Zyklon-B was used for killing.

Organizing genocide

At the Wannsee Conference, held on 20 January 1942, the SS secured the full cooperation of top German civil servants for their cold-blooded genocide. They needed this support because the organization of the Final Solution posed enormous problems. Adolf Eichmann was put in charge of arranging the transport of Jews from all over Europe to the gas chambers in the east. He had to make sure that trains were available

Adolf Eichmann.

Being rounded up in the Warsaw ghetto, 1943 (top); and (bottom) boarding a deportation train.

when needed, that the right number of Jews turned up for transportation, and that the death camps had the capacity to 'process' – that is, exterminate – the number of Jews he was sending.

'A life-and-death struggle'

In March 1942, the German propaganda minister Joseph Goebbels wrote about the extermination of the Jews in his diary:

'One cannot afford sentimentality in a situation such as this. The Jews would destroy us if we did not defend ourselves. It's a life-and-death struggle between the Aryan race and the Jewish bacillus. No other government, and no other regime, could summon the strength for such a general solution to this question.'

Joseph Goebbels was the leading Nazi propagandist. He worked up hate campaigns against the Jews.

Where possible, the Nazis made sure that Jews played a part in organizing their own destruction. Jewish leaders were appointed to run the ghettos and were made responsible for selecting people for transport to the camps. They also had to ensure that those selected turned up at the transportation points at the allotted time. The whole operation was financed by money taken from Jewish people.

In early 1942, the trains began to arrive daily at the extermination camps. First were Jews from the Polish ghettos and the German Reich. Then transports began to arrive from all over Europe – from France, the Netherlands, Belgium, Norway and Croatia. By August the gas chambers at Treblinka and Belzec alone were killing 140,000 people a month.

The darkest chapter

Some Jewish writers have controversially attacked Jewish leaders for cooperating with the Nazis in carrying out the Holocaust. American Jewish author Hannah Arendt wrote:

'To a Jew this role of the Jewish leaders in the destruction of their own people is undoubtedly the darkest chapter of the whole dark story ... In Amsterdam as in Warsaw, in Berlin as in Budapest, Jewish officials could be trusted to compile the list of persons and of their property, to secure money from the deportees to defray the expenses of their deportation and extermination, to keep track of vacated apartments, to supply police forces to help seize Jews and get them on trains, until, as a last gesture, they handed over the assets of the Jewish community in good order for final confiscation.' (From *Eichmann in Jerusalem*)

However, the Jewish leaders were obviously in an appalling situation. They felt powerless to resist the Nazis directly. Most cooperated in the hope of saving at least some Jewish lives.

Indescribable suffering

The Nazis always spoke of the Jews as a dangerous enemy threatening the German people, but in reality Jews were easy victims. They were defenceless. They had no government, no army and no weapons. Constant hunger and fear reduced most to a state of passive despair. Few resisted or attempted to escape when they were rounded up to be taken to the camps. Many, feeling they had nowhere to hide, simply presented themselves at the station at the appointed time for the train, bringing with them what possessions they could carry.

The journey to a camp was often a form of torture. Crowded into goods wagons without food or drink for days on end, people offered their guards watches and jewels in exchange for a cup of water. Many died in the

A memorial to Janus Korczak, at the Yad V'Shem museum of the Holocaust in Jerusalem. Korczak was a Polish educator and educational theorist who voluntarily accompanied the children from his orphanage when they were deported.

wagons. The arrival at the camp brought no relief. Those who were not immediately gassed were plunged into the terrifying routines of camp life. The Nazis had no intention that those selected for work should survive. They were intended for a slow death instead of a quick one.

Deathly secret

The Nazis did everything in their power to keep the extermination programme a secret. The death camps were located in remote areas in the east. Most people knew that the Jews were being deported eastward, but it was possible to hide the fact that the destination of most was instant death. In letters and documents, the Nazis never used such words as 'extermination' or 'killing'. Instead, they used code words such as 'final solution', 'evacuation', or 'special treatment'.

When the war ended, Adolf Eichmann escaped and started a new life in Argentina. But in 1960 he was kidnapped and taken to Jerusalem where he was tried for war crimes. This photograph was taken at his trial.

The very enormity of the extermination programme made it almost impossible to believe. Even many Jews refused to believe rumours of what was happening, because it made no sense. Why transport people thousands of miles just to kill them? It was easier to believe what they were told – that the trains were carrying Jews to forced labour or resettlement camps.

Efficient destruction

The process of extermination did not always run like clockwork. For example, SS officers wanting to take Jews to the gas chambers often clashed with industrial managers or army officers wanting to use them for work. But the German genius for efficient organization guaranteed that the programme on the whole functioned smoothly.

Many thousands of Germans were involved in the exterminations in an everyday way. Ordinary businesses supplied the gas trucks used at Chelmno

66   Facing reality

Most of the individuals who organized the Holocaust kept as far away as possible from the actual killing. Adolf Eichmann, who played a leading part in sending millions of Jews to their deaths, once witnessed people being killed in gas vans at Chelmno. He later said:

'I hardly looked. I could not; I could not; I had had enough ... the doors were opened, and the corpses were thrown out ... They were hurled into the ditch, and I can still see a civilian extracting the teeth with tooth pliers. And then I was off – jumped into my car and did not open my mouth any more ... I was finished.' (Quoted in H. Arendt, *Eichmann in Jerusalem*)

But Eichmann went on organizing the transport of Jews to the death camps, from a safe distance in his office. 99

Happy arrival at Treblinka

Richard Glazar was one of many Jews who did not believe what he was told about Nazi killings. In October 1942 he was put on a train to Treblinka. Untypically, it was made up of passenger coaches, not goods wagons. Glazar was firmly convinced that he was going to be put to work:

'We got to Treblinka at 3.30 pm. We all crowded to look out of the windows. I saw a green fence, barracks and I heard what sounded like a farm tractor at work. The place looked like a farm. I thought: "This is marvellous, it's going to be work I know something about."' (Quoted in G. Sereny, *Into That Darkness*)

Within hours of arrival in Treblinka, all but a few of the passengers on Glazar's train had been gassed, and he was employed piling up the clothing of the dead.

and the Zyklon-B gas crystals used at Auschwitz. The trains to the death camps were timetabled by ordinary German railway officials and driven by ordinary railway drivers. The Holocaust depended on all such individuals doing their jobs as usual.

Guards at Belsen concentration camp.

Needing the Jews

The extermination of the Jews was of no practical benefit to the German war effort or economy. It would have been more valuable to keep the Jews alive as slave workers. Indeed, many Jews were spared, at least temporarily, because of their usefulness. Factory managers or army commanders demanded that valuable Jewish workers stay at their posts. Hitler's propaganda chief, Joseph Goebbels, complained in his diary in March 1941:

'We have to go easy on the 30,000 Jews who work in armaments production; we need them – who would have thought this could ever become possible?'

Priority for the Holocaust

By the autumn of 1943, Germany was losing the war, and needed to devote every ounce of its strength to fighting the enemy armies. Yet the Nazis continued to give priority to the search for Jews to kill. The majority of Polish and German Jews were dead. But many Jews remained scattered across Occupied Europe – for example, in Greece, in Hungary and in Italy. Many prayed for deliverance from their oppressors, but no help came and the killing went on.

Disobeying orders

It has often been said that Germans who took part in the slaughter of Jews had to do it, because otherwise they would themselves have been killed. But a former SS officer, Albert Hartl, has said this is untrue. He described how a commander of a task force ordered to massacre Jews

'disapproved of these mass shootings, and therefore had himself transferred as soon as possible from the command ... As far as I know no serious consequences resulted from this ... Concerning the lesser ranks, I also know of no instance in which refusal to take part in the shooting of Jews resulted in any one being sent to a concentration camp or being sentenced to death.' (Quoted in M. Burleigh and W. Wipperman, *The Racial State*)

SURVIVAL AND RESISTANCE

The chances of survival for Jews were not the same in different camps. At Treblinka, Sobibor and Belzec, there were only a few hundred Jewish workers. The hundreds of thousands who arrived at these camps mostly survived for no more than an hour or two. Treblinka was run by only twenty SS men, aided by Ukrainian and Lithuanian guards. The only Jews spared instant death there were those with craft skills useful to the Nazis and those selected to do the work around the gas chambers.

Auschwitz, by contrast, was a huge complex of camps, the size of a city. Its population rose to around 100,000. The gassings took place at Auschwitz-Birkenau. The rest of the camp provided labour for large factories, including the IG Farben Buna rubber plant. The inhabitants of Auschwitz included German political prisoners – socialists and communists – who were better treated than the Jews. There were many more survivors from Auschwitz than from any other camps used for extermination.

Auschwitz was the largest concentration camp ever. About 80 per cent of the people arriving there were sent straight to the gas chambers. The rest went to the labour camp.

Worked to death

A sign over the gates of Auschwitz said 'Arbeit Macht Frei' – Work Makes Free. But life for the Jewish slave workers was an unbroken nightmare. Food was a few pieces of bread and some thin soup. For hours before daybreak, even in the bitterly freezing winter cold, the workers had to stand in inspection parades, often barefoot. Anyone who collapsed or showed any sign of weakness would be 'selected' for gassing. Then the workers were marched off to backbreaking tasks. They were constantly harassed by guards who beat them if they seemed at all slow or clumsy. After a few months of this routine, most camp inmates died of disease or starvation, or were gassed. A small number found a survivable job, in the camp kitchens, for example, or in one of the barrack warehouses where the plunder from the Jewish dead was piled up – clothes, valuables, glasses, shoes and hair.

At Belsen concentration camp the boots of the dead were used as fuel for the living.

The most horrifying fate in the death camps was to be chosen as one of the Special Kommandos. These were the prisoners who worked in and around the gas chambers. Day after day, they helped direct the unsuspecting new arrivals to undress and walk passively into the chamber. Day after day, they pulled the bodies out when the killing was done and searched mouths for gold teeth. They buried the bodies in pits, or fed them into the crematorium furnaces. And they did all this in the knowledge that they themselves would soon be 'processed' in the same way. Periodically, the Special Kommandos were gassed and replaced with a new set of Jews.

Extreme suffering

Some Jews were chosen for medical experiments. Dr Josef Mengele at Auschwitz was the most notorious of many doctors who used Jews for experiments in everything from sterilization to survival under extreme conditions. No anaesthetics were used and suffering was often extreme.

Casual sadism was part of life in all the camps. Kurt Franz, an SS officer at Treblinka, staged boxing matches between Jews in which the contestants had to fight until one of them was dead. The Nazis found it amusing to form Jewish musicians into camp bands to play tunes while the other inmates marched to work or filed towards the gas chambers.

Top: The victim of an experiment at Dachau on the subject of air pressure and parachute jumping.
Right: A survivor of Auschwitz shows pictures of herself and her twin. The only children to survive at Auschwitz were twins, because Mengele had a special interest in the genetics of twins.

Witnessing an execution

In October 1944, an attempted uprising at Auschwitz was crushed.
Afterwards, the prisoners were ordered to watch the execution of one of the
rebels. Primo Levi was one of the witnesses:

'We remained standing, bent and grey, our heads dropped ... The trapdoor
opened, the body wriggled horribly; the band began playing again and we
were once more lined up and filed past the quivering body of the dying man.
At the foot of the gallows, the SS watched us pass with indifferent eyes ...'
(From *If This Is A Man*)

A picture of an execution,
painted by an inmate of
Auschwitz.

Each camp had its whipping post for the punishment
of those who broke any of the camp's thousand minor
rules. Those found guilty of more serious offences,
such as attempting to escape, were hanged in front of
the other prisoners. Some guards would incite their
dogs to savage Jews, for nothing but amusement.

Beatings at Majdanek

Alexander Donat survived the camp at Majdanek. He later wrote:

'Beating and being beaten were taken for granted at Majdanek ... Anyone could beat an inmate and the more experienced inmates never questioned why. They knew that they were beaten merely because they happened to run into someone who wanted to beat them ... The victim was expected to take his licks standing rigidly at attention. Attempts to avoid blows, to cover one's face or head, were treated as additional offences.' (Quoted in D.L. Niewyk, *The Holocaust*)

Auschwitz was surrounded by barbed wire and an electric fence, and the paths were always lit.

Garden at Auschwitz

The camp commandant, Rudolf Hoess, had a very different experience of Auschwitz from the prisoners. While organizing mass murder, Hoess liked to spend time with his family in their pretty house at the camp. He wrote in his memoirs:

'My family, to be sure, were well provided for in Auschwitz. Every wish that my wife or children expressed was granted them ... My wife's garden was a paradise of flowers. The prisoners never missed an opportunity for doing a little act of kindness to my wife or children ... Today I deeply regret that I did not devote more time to my family.' (From *Commandant of Auschwitz*)

Casual brutality

The SS could inflict any casual violence they wished on inmates of the camps. An Auschwitz survivor, Dunja Wasserstrom, witnessed one especially brutal attack by two SS men, called Boger and Draser. The victim was one of the very few children to live as a prisoner at Auschwitz:

'The child was standing next to the car with his apple and was enjoying himself. Suddenly Boger went over to the boy, grabbed his legs, and smashed his head against the wall. Then he calmly picked up the apple. And Draser told me to wipe "that" off the wall.' (Quoted in O. Friedrich, *The Kingdom of Auschwitz*)

Heroic resistance

Resistance inside the camps seemed almost impossible. Survival alone required a superhuman effort. But there were some heroic uprisings. At Treblinka, in August 1943, the prisoners seized weapons from the camp arsenal, killed some of the guards and set fire to the camp buildings. About 150 escaped, although some were later tracked down and killed. At Sobibor, about 300 Jews broke out in October 1943 after attacking their guards with knives and axes. Many escapers survived the war. At Auschwitz there was also a brief, unsuccessful revolt.

Quiet heroism

Many Jews showed sublime courage and heroism in the face of their dreadful fate. Matilda Bandet, a 24-year-old woman from Cracow, Poland, was warned that she and her family were about to be transported to a death camp. She refused to flee, however, saying:

'My place is with my parents. They need me. They are old. They have no means of defending themselves. If I leave them, they will be alone. I will stay here, with them.' (Quoted in M. Gilbert, *The Holocaust*)

She died with her parents in Belzec.

Fighting back

In April 1943, Jews attempted armed resistance as the SS moved in to destroy the Warsaw ghetto. One Jewish fighter, Zivia Lubetkin, later described the exhilaration when they first drew blood:

'When the Germans came up to our posts and marched by and we threw those hand grenades and bombs, and saw German blood pouring over the streets of Warsaw, after we saw so much Jewish blood running in the streets of Warsaw before that, there was rejoicing. The tomorrow did not worry us. The rejoicing amongst Jewish fighters was great and, see the wonder and the miracle, those German heroes retreated, afraid and terrorized from the Jewish bombs and hand grenades, home-made.' (Quoted in M. Gilbert, *The Holocaust*)

The fighting continued for three weeks. Over 7,000 Jews died in the battle.

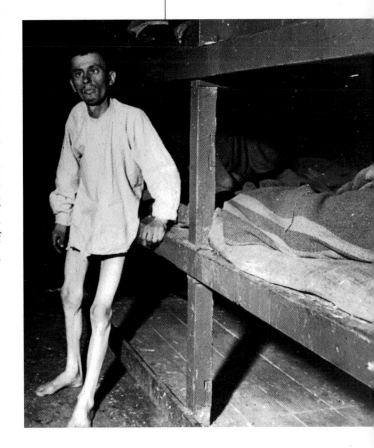

Outside the camps, there were other heroic acts of Jewish resistance. In April 1943, poorly armed Jewish fighters took on the might of the SS in an uprising in the Warsaw ghetto. They were inevitably crushed. In the Soviet Union, some of the Jews who escaped the massacres joined fighting bands in the forests and marshes. About one tenth of the large Soviet partisan movement was Jewish.

A prisoner by his bunk at Buchenwald concentration camp. Prisoners were reduced to such a state of weakness and terror that resistance was almost impossible.

'No apologies are possible'

Historians have asked how much the German people knew about the Holocaust. Albert Speer, Hitler's armaments minister, always claimed that he did not know about it. But, writing in 1970, he denied that this was an excuse:

'Whether I knew or did not know, or how much or how little I knew, is totally unimportant when I consider what horrors I ought to have known about ... No apologies are possible.'
(Quoted in S. Justman, *Holocaust for Beginners*)

Perhaps the same could be said of many Germans: they took care not to enquire what was being done in their name.

Albert Speer, 1971. At the Nuremberg trials in 1945-6, Speer was the only one of the more important Nazi leaders who actually pleaded guilty to war crimes. He was jailed for twenty years. He donated part of the profits from the sales of his memoirs to Jewish organizations.

The response of other Germans

In their extreme predicament, the Jews received very little help from Germans. Despite the secrecy surrounding the Final Solution, most Germans at least knew that the Jews were being treated with extreme cruelty. Thousands saw the trains carrying Jewish people to the camps. Ordinary soldiers in the German army knew all about the massacres in the Soviet Union. Many witnessed some of the terrible scenes at the extermination camps which they passed on trains carrying them to the front. These soldiers told what they had seen to relatives at home. Rumours about gassing were widespread.

Oscar Schindler, a Catholic German factory owner, worked tirelessly to protect Jews when he could and was probably responsible for the survival of around 1,500 individuals. But he was a rare exception. There were virtually no German protests against the treatment of the Jews. Ordinary Germans had shown that they could affect Nazi policies. In 1941, protests by German Catholics had forced the Nazis to halt the gassing of the mentally disabled. On another occasion, when Jews who had married German women were picked up for deportation, the wives demonstrated outside SS offices, demanding their husbands' release. Surprisingly, the men were set free. Yet this was almost the only instance of Germans taking a public stand against the Final Solution.

Protection and betrayal in Occupied Europe

In many parts of Western Europe people made an effort to halt or hinder what was being done to the Jews. Many individuals risked their lives to protect them, allowing them to hide in attics and under floorboards. Some Jews, such as Anne Frank and her family in the Netherlands, stayed in hiding for years.

Anne Frank (right centre), with her father Otto. The diary Anne wrote while the family was in hiding in the Netherlands has made her world-famous.

Anne Frank's diary

Anne Frank was the young daughter of a Jewish banker who emigrated from Germany to the Netherlands to escape Hitler. When the Nazis took over the Netherlands in 1940, the Frank family were trapped. From 1942, for two years, they survived by hiding in a secret annexe to a warehouse. In April 1944, Anne wrote in her diary:

'We have been pointedly reminded that we are in hiding, that we are Jews in chains, chained to one spot, without any rights, with a thousand duties ... Sometime this terrible war will be over. Surely the time will come when we are people again, and not just Jews!'

The Frank family were finally discovered and sent to Auschwitz. Anne Frank died at Belsen camp in 1945.

On the other hand, in all countries, there were individuals who betrayed Jews to the Germans. In Poland, despite the vile treatment the Poles themselves received from the Nazis, hatred of Jews remained widespread.

In Western Europe, the Nazis were dependent on the cooperation of national governments and police forces. In France, for example, French gendarmes rounded up Jews who were not French citizens and put them on trains to Auschwitz. But official opposition to the Final Solution did sometimes slow down the killings. Two of Germany's allies in the war, Hungary and Italy, refused to hand over their Jews for extermination. The Italian government of Benito Mussolini even extended its protection to thousands of French Jews. Both countries were eventually occupied by the Germans – Italy in 1943 and Hungary in 1944 – and after this their Jews were rounded up for slaughter.

Denmark, which was occupied by the Germans in 1940, offered the most successful resistance to the Holocaust. The Danish king demanded to be the first person to wear a yellow star, should the Germans insist on introducing it in Denmark. They never did. In 1943, when it became known that the Germans intended to round up the 8,000 Danish Jews, almost all of them were hidden by local people and ferried across to safety in neutral Sweden.

Two Danish fishermen who made ten crossings to Sweden in October 1943, to take Danish Jews to safety.

A faked funeral

Steffen Lund, a Danish doctor, remembers helping Jewish people escape:

'We had hidden 20 Jews in Bispebjerg Hospital in Copenhagen during the night, when it was surrounded by German police troops and Danish followers. The situation was somewhat discouraging, but we managed to fake a funeral procession, which included 20-30 taxis filled with Jews. We left through a back gate and happily got away with it!'

A cry for help

Although the Nazis tried to keep the Holocaust a secret, it was soon known outside German-occupied Europe that the Jews were being annihilated. A Polish Jew who had fled to London, Szmul Zygielbojm, spoke on BBC radio in July 1942. He called on the world

'to ponder over the undiluted horror of the planned extermination of a whole people ... The governments of Great Britain and America must be compelled to put an end to this mass murder. For if we do not try to find a means of stopping it, we shall bear part of the moral responsibility for what is happening.' (Quoted in G. Sereny, *Into That Darkness*)

Telling the world

Brave individuals carried news of the massacres in Europe to the outside world, but the Allied governments fighting Germany did little to help the Jews. On 17 December 1942, the Allies officially condemned the extermination of the Jews and affirmed their 'solemn resolution to insure that those reponsible for these crimes shall not escape retribution ...'. But they failed to take specific action, such as bombing the railways leading to Auschwitz. A cynical offer by the Nazis in 1944 to exchange Jews for trucks was, not unnaturally, rejected.

The USA did set up a War Refugee Board which, towards the end of the war, helped many Jews to escape. Aiding the Jews was not given high priority, however. Newspapers and official publications in Allied countries did not give the exterminations much publicity. The pope, Pius XII, although fully informed of the killings, made only one veiled reference to the fate of the Jews during the whole war.

In the end, the only hope for the Jews was an Allied victory. By 1944, it seemed certain that Germany was going to be beaten. But for hundreds of thousands more Jews, the end of the war would come too late.

THE LAST ACT

By the autumn of 1943 it was clear to most people that Germany was going to lose the war. The Soviet army was advancing from the east towards the Nazis' secret extermination camps. The SS knew that the killings they had carried out were criminal acts. They began to destroy the evidence of mass murder.

The camps at Treblinka, Sobibor and Belzec were evacuated. Bodies that had been buried were exhumed and burned to ashes. The gas installations were demolished. All remaining Jewish prisoners were killed, so they could not bear witness to what had happened. At Treblinka, a farm was built on the site of the camp and a Ukrainian farmer was installed there. He was told to tell anyone who asked that his family had farmed the property for generations.

The gas chambers at Auschwitz-Birkenau continued to function. The Italian Jews were taken there for extermination from late 1943, the Jews of Greece in spring 1944, the Hungarian Jews between May and July, and the Jews from the Lodz ghetto in August.

On a death march

Raizl Kibel survived one of the death marches in the winter of 1944-5. She later described the horror:

'In a frost, half-barefoot, or entirely barefoot, with light rags upon their emaciated and exhausted bodies, tens of thousands of human creatures drag themselves along in the snow. Only the great, strong striving for life, and the light of imminent liberation, kept them on their feet ... But woe to them whose physical strength abandons them. They are shot on the spot. In such a way were thousands who had endured camp life up to the last minute murdered, a moment before liberation.' (Quoted in M. Gilbert, *The Holocaust*)

Then, in November 1944, after over one million people had died there, Himmler ordered an end to the gassings at Auschwitz. The SS began to destroy buildings and documents. Pits full of human remains were grassed over.

Liberating the camps

The Nazis did not succeed in covering up the traces of their crimes. The camp at Majdanek was overrun by the advancing Soviet army in July 1944. At the end of January 1945, the Soviets liberated Auschwitz. By then, all but 6,000 inmates who were too ill to move had been evacuated by the Nazis. In the Auschwitz storerooms, the Soviets found immediate evidence of mass murder – 836,255 women's coats and dresses and seven tonnes of hair.

As the Germans retreated, they moved their prisoners to camps further west. Hundreds of thousands from Auschwitz and other sites were forced to march great distances in the middle of winter. Thousands died before arriving at camps in the heart of Germany, such as Buchenwald and Bergen-Belsen.

A Hungarian Jew photographed after the liberation of Belsen.

Belsen had been a relatively minor camp. It was suddenly swamped with tens of thousands of new inmates, many from Auschwitz. No food or water was supplied. Typhus broke out and decimated the population of starving prisoners. Rats fed on the thousands of unburied bodies.

Liberating Belsen

Patrick Gordon-Walker, a British journalist, described the scenes as British soldiers liberated the Belsen camp in April 1945:

'The people crowded around them kissing their hands and feet – and dying from weakness. Corpses in every state of decay were lying around, piled up on top of each other in heaps ... People were falling dead all around, people who were walking skeletons. One woman came up to a soldier who was ... doling the milk out to children, and begged for milk for her baby. The man took the baby and saw that it had been dead for days ...' (Quoted in Carey, *The Faber Book of Reportage*)

An SS officer at Belsen, about to make a statement for British Movietone News.

The British army liberated Belsen in April 1945 and the camp was filmed and photographed. For most of the world, these pictures provided the first and most lasting view of the Holocaust.

The first newsreels

George MacDonald Fraser was a soldier who served in Burma during the Second World War. He describes going to a cinema with fellow soldiers at the end of the war and seeing newsreel footage of Belsen:

'We were not a squeamish group in Nine Section; if anyone had seen war in the raw, we had, but that newsreel left us numb. If we hadn't seen those ghastly walking skeletons and great heaps of emaciated bodies, I don't think we'd have believed it. Even now it doesn't seem possible that human behaviour could sink to such depths. Some people left the cinema and one woman was physically sick.' (From *Quartered Safe Out Here*)

A Russian forced labourer points out a German guard who beat and maltreated captives.

In the last months of the war, many of the Nazis most responsible for the Holocaust planned their escape. They organized false identity papers and burned incriminating documents. But Himmler was one of many captured by the Allies. He committed suicide. Hitler also killed himself, in his Berlin bunker, on 30 April 1945.

Hitler's last testament

Facing defeat in April 1945, Hitler claimed that the Jews had been responsible for the war, and he gloried in his bid to exterminate them. Comparing the First World War with the Second, he said:

'I left no one in doubt that this time not only would millions of children of European Aryan races starve, not only would millions of grown men meet their death ... but this time the real culprits [the Jews] would have to pay for their guilt even though by more humane means than war.' (Quoted in M. Gilbert, *The Holocaust*)

By 'more humane means', Hitler meant the gas chambers.

CRYING OUT FOR JUSTICE

Germans were made to confront what had been happening in the camps run by their compatriots.

During the war, the Allies had promised to try war criminals. They kept their promise. At the Nuremberg trials in 1945-6, twenty-four of the main Nazi leaders were tried for crimes against humanity. Twelve were sentenced to death. Hermann Goering committed suicide to avoid hanging. The trial of many lesser figures in Hitler's regime followed.

But the Allies' enthusiasm for punishing Germans soon faded. Individuals who had played a key role in the Final Solution rarely served more than five years in prison. Industrialists who had profited from Jewish slave labour either received token prison sentences or went scot free. Many individuals who had taken an active part in the Holocaust either escaped to South America or discreetly resumed ordinary lives in Germany or Austria. Some once more reached high positions in the state or economic life.

The birth of Israel

The Nazis had killed six million Jews, three quarters of all the Jews who had been living in Europe in 1939. The remaining European Jews tried to rebuild their lives. Most had lost their homes and the communities they once lived in. They wished to emigrate, but the USA and Britain were not prepared

Dissatisfied with the Nuremberg verdicts, demonstrators in 1946 called for all Nazi leaders to be punished by death.

Just obeying orders

After the war, Nazis who were charged with crimes against humanity repeatedly claimed that they had just been obeying orders. For example, Rudolf Hoess, the commandant of Auschwitz, defended carrying out the order to gas the Jews:

'It was certainly an extraordinary and monstrous order. Nevertheless, the reasons behind the extermination programme seemed to me right. I did not reflect on it at the time; I had been given an order, and I had to carry it out. Whether this mass extermination of the Jews was necessary or not was something on which I could not allow myself to form an opinion ...'
(From *Commandant of Auschwitz*)

Hoess was executed for his crimes in 1947.

Hermann Goering at the Nuremberg courthouse. He committed suicide in 1946, to avoid punishment by hanging.

New immigrants to Israel directed to the milk station and showers of a transit camp reception station.

to accept more than a small number. Thousands found their way to Palestine, despite attempts by the British authorities there to stop them entering. In 1948 the Jewish state of Israel was created in Palestine and opened its arms to European Jews.

Millions of Jews who had escaped or survived the Holocaust had lost some or all of their relatives, and yet did not know exactly how or where they had met their dreadful fate. The survivors were haunted by their memories. Many felt guilt at having survived when so many others had died.

The Auschwitz camp markings made on people's arms were impossible to remove.

In the 1950s, to a large extent, the world, and especially Germany, tried to forget the Holocaust. It was blamed on the Nazis, who were a thing of the past. West Germany paid reparations on a vast scale to Israel, but the Holocaust was not mentioned in West German school history books. Most of the property stolen from murdered Jews was dispersed, with little attempt to locate relatives of the original owners.

Simon Wiesenthal was one Jewish investigator in particular who was tireless in bringing the guilty to justice.

Crimes unearthed

But the Holocaust was an event that refused to be consigned to history and forgotten. In 1960, Israeli agents kidnapped Adolf Eichmann, who had started a new life in Argentina. He was carried off to Jerusalem for trial. Soon, many other ex-Nazis were being tracked down and prosecuted, from Franz Stangl, the commandant of Treblinka, to sadistic Ukrainian camp guards.

The generation of Germans who grew up in the 1960s and 1970s were horrified at what their parents had done. They denounced university professors still in place who had preached racist doctrines during the Nazi period, and bureaucrats who had organized the Holocaust and were still in office.

Eichmann on trial

The trial of Adolf Eichmann in Jerusalem in 1961-2 gave new insight into the mentality behind the Holocaust. Eichmann was far from being a sadistic brute. He was a mild-mannered, rather boring bureaucrat. Denying murder, he said with obvious sincerity:

'With the killing of Jews I had nothing to do. I never killed a Jew, or a non-Jew for that matter – I never killed any human being.'

Yet Eichmann had coordinated the delivery of millions of Jews to the gas chambers. That was his job, which he did as well as he could. He took pride in his efficiency, which he naively thought the court might hold in his favour. The sheer dullness of Eichmann led author Hannah Arendt to describe him as a lesson in 'the fearsome, word-and-thought-defying banality of evil.'

The revelation of the crimes the Nazis had committed helped to discredit racism around the world. And yet there were political groups in many countries that continued to advocate racist ideas. Some adopted Nazi emblems such as the swastika. Admirers of Hitler even tried to claim that the Holocaust never happened.

The next generation

In the 1960s, young Germans became aware of the hideous crimes that their parents' generation had committed. Edda Bohnsack recalls first learning of the Holocaust when she was 12 years old:

'My reaction was sheer horror at what we, the Germans, had done. I began to have rows with my parents. I asked them why they didn't do anything to stop it, why they let it happen ... Later, when I began to travel abroad, it was even worse. I had this friend in Australia, and her grandparents were Auschwitz survivors. They were so nice to me. I just wanted to die of guilt and shame.' (From an interview with the author)

Bitter remembrance

More than fifty years after the end of the war, the struggle to uncover the past continues. Every year, some attempt is made to prosecute a now elderly man believed to have once been a murderer of Jews. Property stolen from the Jews is still being tracked down, from paintings now in national art museums to money in Swiss bank accounts. Across Europe, memorials have been raised to the Holocaust victims, so the dead shall not be forgotten.

Triumph of life

A survivor of the Holocaust, Cordelia Edvardson, wrote in 1984:

'I may bear indelible scars in body and soul, but I don't intend to reveal them to the world – least of all to the Germans. That is the pride of the survivor. Hitler is dead – but I am alive.' (Quoted in M. Gilbert, *The Holocaust*)

On the fiftieth anniversary of the liberation of Auschwitz, sixteen heads of state were among the thousands of people who gathered for a moving commemoration. One of these was President Helmut Kohl of Germany. But many Jews resented the call for forgiveness and reconciliation that was the theme of the occasion. One camp survivor, Nobel prize winner Elie Wiesel, prayed: 'God, do not have mercy on those who have created this place. God of forgiveness, do not forgive those murderers of Jewish children here.' The utter darkness of the Holocaust overwhelms our understanding and defies the healing power of time.

The Holocaust memorial
in Miami, Florida.

DATE LIST

1933

30 January   Adolf Hitler becomes chancellor of Germany.

1 April   Nazi stormtroopers enforce a one-day boycott of Jewish-owned shops and businesses.

1935

15 September   The Nuremberg Laws deprive German Jews of their civil rights and ban marriages between Jews and 'Aryans'.

1938

13 March   Germany annexes Austria in the Anschluss. This is followed by widespread attacks on Austria's large Jewish population.

9-10 November   On Krystallnacht (the 'night of broken glass'), synagogues are burned down across Germany and Austria. Jews are attacked and many are carried off to concentration camps.

1939

30 January   Hitler tells the Reichstag (the German parliament) that another war will mean the 'annihilation of the Jewish race in Europe'.

1 September   The Second World War begins in Europe when Germany invades Poland.

23 November   Polish Jews, who have been herded into ghettos, are ordered to wear a yellow star.

1940

January   The Nazis begin a programme of gassing of the mentally disabled in Germany.

1941

22 June   The Germans and their allies invade the Soviet Union in Operation Barbarossa. SS units known as Einsatzgruppen have orders to follow the advancing armies and kill all Soviet Jews.

31 July   Hitler's associate Hermann Goering orders Reinhard Heydrich, second-in-command of the SS, to prepare a 'Final Solution' of the Jewish problem.

28-30 September   Over 33,000 Soviet Jews are massacred and buried in a mass grave at Babi Yar, outside Kiev.

November   The Nazis begin Operation Reinhard. They plan to transport all Polish Jews to death camps and exterminate them.

1942

20 January   At the Wannsee Conference, Heydrich tells heads of German government departments of the part they must play in the 'Final Solution'.

February   The mass deportation of Jews from Western Europe for extermination in the death camps begins.

17 December   The Western Allies publicly denounce the massacre of the Jewish people, but fail to do anything about it.

1943

19 April   An uprising in the Jewish ghetto in Warsaw begins. It is crushed by the Germans.

2 August	A prisoners' uprising at Treblinka extermination camp partially succeeds. The gas chambers there are destroyed.

1944

April-July	The Germans take control of Hungary and deport 437,000 Hungarian Jews, nearly 300,000 of them to the gas chambers at Auschwitz.
24 July	Soviet troops liberate the death camp at Majdanek and uncover evidence of mass murder.
27 November	SS head Heinrich Himmler orders an end to gassing at Auschwitz, the last functioning death camp.

1945

27 January	Soviet troops liberate Auschwitz.
April	Allied forces overrun camps at Belsen, Buchenwald and Dachau.
30 April	Hitler commits suicide in his Berlin bunker

RESOURCES

RECOMMENDED READING

Hannah Arendt, *Eichmann in Jerusalem*, Penguin, 1994: Originally written in the early 1960s, this book gradually takes apart the strange personality of the Nazi bureaucrat Adolf Eichmann.

Martin Gilbert, *The Holocaust*, Fontana, 1989: by far the fullest account, from the point of view of the victims. It is packed with heart-rending accounts – a long, tough book, but well worth reading.

Robert Harris, *Fatherland*, Arrow Books, 1992: a best-seller which explores what might have happened if the Nazis had won the war and completed their project for the Holocaust.

Philip Kerr, *Berlin Noir*, Penguin, 1992: a series of three detective novels set in Nazi Germany. They are a good read and carry a fair amount of information about the Nazi police state and its brutality.

Thomas Keneally, *Schindler's Ark*, Hodder and Stoughton, 1982: a gripping 'faction' novel about Oscar Schindler, a businessman who saved the lives of his Jewish workers during the Holocaust.

Primo Levi, *If This Is A Man*, Abacus, 1993: the most harrowing first-hand account of life in Auschwitz, written by an Italian survivor.

FILMS

Au Revoir les Enfants is a touching film by the French director, Louis Malle, about a Jewish boy hiding in a French Catholic school during the Nazi occupation of France.

Schindler's List by Steven Spielberg is an Oscar-winning epic movie about the Holocaust, based on the book *Schindler's Ark*.

Shoah by Claude Lanzmann is a film you are unlikely to watch right through, since it lasts nine hours and consists entirely of interviews with people who witnessed the Holocaust at first hand. Yet no other film has captured half as much of the reality of the Holocaust. Perhaps try to find it in a video store and watch an hour now and then.

The Odessa File, based on the best-seller by Frederick Forsyth, is a thriller about the hunt for a Nazi war criminal living prosperously in post-war Germany.

GLOSSARY

Anschluss   union of Austria with Germany. This had been forbidden by the Treaty of Versailles, but was achieved when Hitler annexed Austria to the German Reich in March 1938.

anti-Semitism   hatred of, or prejudice against, Jews.

Aryan race   according to Hitler (who based his ideas on some nineteenth-century racial theories), a superior race of which Germans were the purest example. He argued that the Jews were trying to corrupt the Aryan race, in order to conquer the world.

concentration camp   a prison camp set up to hold people considered a danger to the state, perhaps because of the political group to which they belong. The British held people in concentration camps during the Boer War (1899-1902). The first Nazi concentration camps were set up in 1933, for communists and other opponents of the Nazi Party.

Einsatz-gruppen   SS task forces who followed the German armies as they invaded Poland, the Baltic States and the USSR, rounding up and killing the Jews in the conquered areas.

genocide   the deliberate destruction of a racial, religious, political or ethnic group.

ghetto   part of a city within which Jews were forced by law to stay, separated from the rest of the population. The word 'ghetto' was first used in Venice in 1516.

Nuremberg Laws   laws announced at the Nazi rally at Nuremberg in September 1935 which took citizenship away from Jews and forbade them to marry Germans.

Nuremberg trials   a series of trials of Nazis before a tribunal of British, French, Soviet and US judges. In the first trial (Nov. 1945-Oct. 1946), 12 were sentenced to death, 7 received long prison sentences and 3 were acquitted. A further 12 trials were held, of another 177 people.

partisans   resistance fighters in Poland, the USSR, Yugoslavia and Italy.

pogrom   an organized attack on Jews, either approved or condoned by the authorities.

racism   the belief that some races are naturally superior to others and so have the right to dominate and discriminate against them.

SA (Sturm-abteilung)   'assault division' founded by Hitler in 1921. Known as stormtroopers or 'brownshirts', they protected Nazi Party meetings and attacked political opponents, especially communists. By 1933 there were 2 million SA members and they freely carried out violent attacks on Jews. In 1934 Hitler realized that he needed to reduce the organization's power, in order to gain the support of the army and industrialists, and so he had the SA leaders killed.

SS (Schutz-staffel)   'protective squad' founded in 1925 as Hitler's personal bodyguard. From 1929 Heinrich Himmler built it into a 250,000-strong organization with huge police and military powers. It was responsible for concentration camps and racial matters. At the Nuremberg trials it was declared a criminal organization.

INDEX

SOURCES

The quotations in this book were taken from:
Hannah Arendt, *Eichmann in Jerusalem*, Penguin, 1994
Michael Burleigh and Wolfgang Wipperman, *The Racial State*, Cambridge University Press, 1991
John Carey, ed., *The Faber Book of Reportage*, London and Boston, 1987
Anne Frank, *The Diary of Anne Frank*, Viking, 1989
George MacDonald Fraser, *Quartered Safe Out Here*, Harvill, 1992
Otto Friedrich, *The Kingdom of Auschwitz*, Penguin, 1995
Martin Gilbert, *The Holocaust*, Fontana, 1989
Hermann Graml, *Anti-Semitism in the Third Reich*, Blackwell, 1992
Raul Hilberg, *The Destruction of the European Jews*, W. H. Allen, 1961
Rudolf Hoess, *Commandant of Auschwitz*, Weidenfeld, 1959
Stewart Justman, *Holocaust for Beginners*, Writers and Readers Publishing, 1995
Primo Levi, *If This Is A Man*, Abacus, 1993
Louis P. Lochner, ed., *The Goebbels Diaries*, New York, 1948
Donald L. Niewyk, ed., *The Holocaust*, Heath and Co., 1992
Gitta Sereny, *Into That Darkness: From Mercy Killing to Mass Murder*, Pimlico, 1995